Healing

Forever Settled

Healing
Forever Settled

Kenneth W. Hagin

Unless otherwise indicated, all Scripture quotations are taken from the *King James Version* of the Bible.

20 19 18 17 16 15 14   14 13 12 11 10 09 08

Healing—Forever Settled
ISBN-13: 978-0-89276-723-6
ISBN-10: 0-89276-723-5

In the U.S. write:
Kenneth Hagin Ministries
P.O. Box 50126
Tulsa, OK 74150-0126
1-888-28-FAITH
rhema.org

In Canada write:
Kenneth Hagin Ministries of Canada
P.O. Box 335, Station D
Etobicoke (Toronto), Ontario
Canada M9A 4X3
1-866-70-Rhema
rhemacanada.org

Contents

—Chapter 1—

Healing in Redemption: A Present-Tense Reality

Probably one of the most paramount questions believers ask today is whether or not it is God's will to heal. The question is not whether God is *able* to heal sickness and disease, but whether God is *willing* to heal sickness and disease.

Is it God's will to heal? The answer is *most assuredly, yes!* The Bible tells us that healing is the will of God. Healing is a forever-settled subject because *God's Word* is forever settled.

PSALM 119:89
89 For ever, 0 Lord, thy word is settled in heaven.

The Bible tells us that God dealt with the sin problem of humanity by sending His Son Jesus to be a Sacrifice and a Substitute for us. Isaiah 53:5 says, ". . . *he* [Jesus] *was wounded for our transgressions, he was bruised for our iniquities.*" And First Peter 2:24 says. *"Who his own self bare our sins in his own body on the tree. . . ."* But both of these scriptures *also* state that God dealt with *sickness and disease* for us in Christ's great substitutionary work on the Cross.

ISAIAH 53:4–5
4 Surely he hath borne our griefs [sicknesses or diseases], **and carried our sorrows** [pains]: **yet we did esteem him stricken, smitten of God, and afflicted.**

5 But he was wounded for our transgressions, he was bruised for our iniquities: the chastisement of our peace was upon him; and WITH HIS STRIPES WE ARE HEALED.

1

Verse 5 says, "...*with his stripes we ARE HEALED.*" It does not say we *might* be healed or that we *are going to be* healed at some time in the future. No, the Bible says we are healed! That's present tense. That means healing is a reality right now. With His stripes we are healed! Healing is a present-tense fact which is already established in God's Word.

What does it mean that healing is a present-tense fact? Let me give you an example. Suppose you said to one of your city officials, for instance, to the mayor of your city, "You are the mayor." That means he is presently the mayor, correct? It means he *presently* stands in that office and holds that title. If he were only running for the office of mayor, but you believed he was going to win the election, you might say, "You *are going* to be the next mayor." Or you could say, "You *might* be the next mayor." But if he were already standing in that office and holding the title of mayor, that means he is the mayor *now*.

In the same way, God states a present-tense fact about us in His Word. His Word declares what we are *right now!* He says, "You *are* healed." That's present, not future tense. Isaiah penned these words in Isaiah 53:4–5 by the inspiration of the Holy Spirit even before Jesus came to earth in the flesh to redeem mankind. Therefore, in the mind of God, the work of redemption was already an established fact.

Let's look at the New Testament counterparts of Isaiah 53:4–5.

MATTHEW 8:16–17

16 When the even was come, they brought unto him [Jesus] **many that were possessed with devils: and he cast out the spirits with his word, and healed all that were sick:**

17 That it might be fulfilled which was spoken by Esaias [Isaiah] **the prophet, saying, HIMSELF TOOK OUR INFIRMITIES, and BARE OUR SICKNESSES.**

1 PETER 2:24

24 Who his own self bare our sins in his own body on the tree, that we, being dead to sins, should live unto righteousness: BY WHOSE STRIPES YE WERE HEALED.

By healing the sick in His earthly ministry (as we saw in Matthew 8:16–17), Jesus was fulfilling Isaiah's prophecy, *". . .with his stripes we are healed,"* before He ever went to the Cross and legally obtained redemption for us. Then the Apostle Peter restates God's will concerning healing in First Peter 2:24: *". . .by whose stripes ye WERE healed."* Peter was an eyewitness to what took place as described by Isaiah. Peter was present when the Roman soldiers put those stripes on Jesus' back and hung Him on the Cross. Because Peter was an eyewitness to the agony Jesus suffered, no wonder he could say along with Isaiah: "With His stripes we were healed"!

According to the Word of God, Jesus not only died and rose again for our sins, but He died and rose again for our sicknesses and diseases too. Healing belongs to us just as salvation belongs to us. *Healing is part and parcel of our redemption.*

Looking at the Psalms, we see again that healing is one of the benefits of redemption.

PSALM 103:1–3

1 **Bless the Lord, O my soul: and all that is within me, bless his holy name.**

2 **Bless the Lord, O my soul, and forget not all his BENEFITS:**

3 **Who FORGIVETH ALL THINE INIQUITIES; who HEALETH ALL THY DISEASES.**

Verse 3 says the Lord heals *all* of our diseases—not just a few—and not just our *minor* ailments. He heals them ALL! The word "all" means *nothing left out*. Nothing is left out of the redemptive work of Christ—not a headache, not a stomachache, not any kind of cancer, nor any kind of heart trouble—not any sickness or disease! In God's plan of redemption, every sickness and disease has been dealt with!

The Willingness of Jesus To Heal

Let's look at another passage of Scripture that further illustrates God's will concerning healing.

LUKE 5:12–13

12 And it came to pass, when he was in a certain city, behold a man full of leprosy: who seeing Jesus fell on his face, and besought him, saying, Lord, if thou wilt, thou canst make me clean.

13 And he put forth his hand, and touched him, saying, I WILL: BE THOU CLEAN. And immediately the leprosy departed from him.

The question concerning God's will to heal is answered very explicitly in this passage of Scripture. When the leper questioned Jesus specifically concerning His will to heal, Jesus answered, "I WILL!" The *New International Version* says. "'Lord, if you are willing, you can make me clean.' Jesus reached out his hand and touched the man. *'I am willing,'* he said. 'Be clean!' And immediately the leprosy left him" (vv. 12–13).

In verse 12 in the *King James Version*, notice it says the man was *full of leprosy,* indicating that the man had leprosy which was in the last stages. Leprosy is a hideous disease which deforms and mutilates the body as it progresses. We can gather from this passage that since the man was *full* of leprosy, the disease was probably more advanced than just a spot on his arm or leg at that point. Yet with one sentence from the Master's lips: *"be thou clean,"* the leper was healed!

As a leper, this man was considered unclean and according to Jewish law, because of his disease he was an outcast. He couldn't live among others who were healthy and whole, and if he was ever in public, he had to cry out, "Unclean! Unclean!" So actually when the leper threw himself at Jesus' feet, he was defying Jewish law and custom and was risking being put to death for breaking the law. But he had heard about Jesus and the miracles He performed, so this leper begged Jesus to heal him. But the point is, when the leper questioned Jesus specifically concerning His willingness to heal him, Jesus answered, "I WILL! BE CLEAN!" (Luke 5:13). *The New English Bible* renders this passage: "Indeed I will; be clean again." From this scripture, we can clearly see that Jesus fully demonstrated His willingness to heal.

It is evident that the leper had heard about the healings Jesus performed because he fell at Jesus' feet, saying, "If you will, you *can* heal me." Therefore, the leper knew Jesus had the power to heal; he never questioned Jesus' *ability* or power to heal. However, the leper did question Jesus' *willingness* to heal. He said, *"Lord, if thou WILT, thou canst make me clean"* (Luke 5:12). But once Jesus settled the question of His willingness to heal by saying, *"I will: be thou clean,"* the leper received his healing and the leprosy departed from him!

Most Christians today don't have a problem seeing Jesus in His earthly ministry as the Healer. They don't question that He was anointed by God and that He had the power to heal sickness and disease. Most Christians don't even question so much Jesus' *ability* to heal people today as they do His *willingness* to demonstrate that healing power on their behalf.

However, any question as to Jesus' willingness to heal is answered very vividly in this account of the leper in Luke chapter 5. And since Jesus hasn't changed, and He was willing to heal then, He is willing to heal now.

HEBREWS 13:8
8 Jesus Christ the same yesterday, and to day, and for ever.

It stands to reason that if Jesus was willing to heal people in His earthly ministry, He is willing to heal us today! We need to have faith not only in Jesus' *power* and *ability* to heal, but also in His *willingness* and *compassion* to heal. We should no longer question whether or not Jesus wants to heal us because He is the same yesterday, today, and forever. He hasn't changed! He is still saying, "I will!"

Developing Unshakable Faith

But once we know the will of God concerning healing—that healing *is* God's will—we can hinder our own prayers with the faith-destroying words, *"If it be Thy will."* To conclude a prayer for healing with the words, "If it be Thy will," when Scripture clearly teaches that it is God's will to heal, is to pray in doubt and unbelief because it means we aren't approaching God on the authority of His written Word. And as long as we are in doubt and unbelief we can't receive healing or *any* blessing from God.

JAMES 1:6–7

6 **But let him ask in faith, nothing wavering. For he that wavereth is like a wave of the sea driven with the wind and tossed.**

7 **For let not that man think that he shall receive any thing of the Lord.**

The reason many people aren't receiving heaven's best is that they're *halfway in* faith and *halfway out* of faith, so to speak. In other words, they aren't really sure what they believe! They're not really committed to the integrity of God's Word. One day you might hear them speaking the Word and shouting the victory, and the next day you might hear them talking doubt and unbelief. But the Bible says here in James chapter 1, that the one who wavers won't receive anything from the Lord.

Your faith in God's Word must be firm and unshakable. You can develop a firm and unshakable faith in God's Word by hearing it, by meditating on it, and by settling in your heart on the absolute integrity of the Word. This is the only way you will obtain faith because the Bible says, *"faith cometh by hearing, and hearing by the word of God"* (Rom. 10:17). When God's Word becomes firmly established in your heart, you'll have no trouble believing God for healing and appropriating it for yourself because God's Word is *forever settled* on the subject of healing.

One way Christians, including ministers of the gospel, demonstrate their lack of faith is when they pray for healing by saying, "*If* it be Thy will." People usually do this because they are basing their prayers on Jesus' prayer to God in the Garden of Gethsemane just before His betrayal and crucifixion. Jesus prayed, *"Father, IF THOU BE WILLING, remove this cup from me: nevertheless not my will, but thine, be done"* (Luke 22:42; *see* also Matt. 26:42,44 and Mark 14:35–36). They conclude that because Jesus prayed that way, then it must be scriptural to pray, "If it be Thy will."

However, in the Garden of Gethsemane Jesus was praying a prayer of consecration—a prayer of commitment to do God's will. That's the only reason He prayed, "If it be Thy will." Jesus said to the Father, "Not My will, but Yours be done." Jesus was in anguish of soul as He prayed, "Father, if You are willing, let this cup pass from Me; nevertheless, not My will, but Yours be done" (Luke 22:42). Jesus' prayer had nothing to do with questioning God's will concerning His willingness to heal. It was a prayer of commitment and dedication to God. Jesus was simply reaffirming His commitment to willingly obey God's will no matter what suffering it would cost Him personally.

You don't have to pray, "If it be Thy will" when God's will is already established and revealed in His Word. You already know God's will concerning healing, for example, because you have His Word for it; you have specific scriptures to base your faith on. God's will concerning healing is plainly stated in His Word. *God's Word is God's will.*

I heard about a young Christian woman who was fasting and praying and seeking God about whether she should marry a certain man who wasn't a Christian. She prayed, "Lord, if it be Your will, let me marry this man." But she already had God's will on the matter because she had God's Word on the matter. The Bible says, *"Be ye not unequally yoked together with unbelievers"* (2 Cor. 6:14). This man was an unbeliever and she was a believer. She didn't need to fast and pray to get God's will; His will was already plainly stated in His Word concerning her situation, and all the fasting and praying in the world wasn't going to change it. It's different when a couple is already married and one of them gets saved: the Bible also addresses that kind of a situation. But according to the Word of God an unmarried Christian is not to marry someone who is unsaved—period!

Certainly we can include the word, "if" when praying about matters where God's will has not been specifically revealed concerning our situation. For example, we may be praying for direction and guidance in a particular area of our own lives. The Bible doesn't give specific direction as to what city we are to live in, for example, or what church we are to belong to. In situations such as these, it would be all right to pray, "If it be Thy will," because the will of God in that situation has not been expressly revealed to us in His Word.

However, when we know what God's Word has to say about our situation, all doubts should be settled. And we certainly don't have to doubt God's will concerning healing because we already have His Word for it! Healing is a forever-settled subject!

—Chapter 2—

Having Faith in
a Faithful God

As a parent, if you tell your children that you're going to give them a gift, and they come to you later begging for what you've already promised them, you'd be upset with them. By their actions they would be saying, "We know you *said* you'd do it, but we don't believe you *will!*" That's basically what we do to Jesus our Healer when we conclude our prayers for healing with the statement, "If it be Thy will." Jesus has already given His Word to us about healing: "With His stripes we are healed!"

Instead of basing our prayers for healing on the way Jesus prayed in the Garden of Gethsemane, "If it be Thy will," why not base our prayers for healing on the way Jesus prayed *for healing?* Actually, if you'll notice how Jesus ministered to sick people in His earthly ministry, you'll find that most of the time He didn't even pray for their healing; He just spoke words to the effect, "Be healed!" and the sick were healed. Jesus did pray, however, when He raised Lazarus from the dead. Jesus said, *"Father, I thank thee THAT THOU HAST HEARD ME"* (John 11:41). Then Jesus commanded, *"Lazarus, COME FORTH"* (v. 43). And if you'll study the different accounts of healing in the four Gospels, you'll notice that Jesus never refused anyone who came to Him to receive healing. Not once will you find Jesus praying to God, "Father, heal this person *if* it be Thy will." Jesus never prayed that way because He already knew God's will on the subject of healing!

Of course, opponents of divine healing will always be able to cite cases of sick people who were prayed for, but didn't receive their healing. When people aren't healed, many automatically conclude, "Well, it must be God's will that I'm sick." But isn't it strange that then they'll make an appointment with the doctor to get some medication so they can get well *and get out of the will of God!* Well, if it's not God's will to heal—if it's God's will for His people to be sick—then according to that kind of thinking, sick people need to pray for more sickness so they can be certain they're in the *perfect* will of God!

You might say, "That sounds ridiculous!" Yes, it certainly does! But I said that to help you see the absurdity of some of the teachings we hear in the Body of Christ today which try to prove that divine healing is not God's will for us, or that it's not for us today.

Healing is God's will because God's Word says it is, and it is impossible for God to lie (Num. 23:19). It is God's will for us to be well, whole, happy, and blessed because the Bible says that God is our heavenly *Father*, and as a father, He loves us and wants only the best for us.

MATTHEW 7:7–11

7 Ask, and it shall be given you; seek, and ye shall find; knock, and it shall be opened unto you:

8 For every one that asketh receiveth; and he that seeketh findeth; and to him that knocketh it shall be opened.

9 Or what man is there of you, whom if his son ask bread, will he give him a stone?

10 Or if he ask a fish, will he give him a serpent?

11 If ye then, being evil [or natural], know how to give good gifts unto your children, HOW MUCH MORE SHALL YOUR FATHER WHICH IS IN HEAVEN GIVE GOOD THINGS TO THEM THAT ASK HIM?

Many people believe that God afflicts people with sickness and disease in order to discipline them or to teach them a lesson. But how many of you who are parents would discipline your children by making them sick? If you could, would you get some cancer and inject it into your children and tell them, "Now, I'm going to teach you a few things"? Of course not! Besides, if you were to do that, I guarantee, you'd spend quite a few years locked up behind bars! Well, the Bible says if natural parents know how to give good gifts to their children, *how much more* does God our heavenly Father know how to give good gifts to *His* children! Yet our heavenly Father is accused of giving His children cancer, tuberculosis, and every other kind of malady and sickness you can think of. That kind of reasoning doesn't even make sense!

JAMES 1:17

17 Every GOOD GIFT and every PERFECT GIFT is from above, and cometh down FROM THE FATHER of lights, with whom is no variableness, neither shadow of turning.

We can readily see from this scripture that it is God who has provided the many ways for us to be helped, healed, and blessed in this natural realm we live in. God does not object to people obtaining healing through natural means—through medical science, for example. But on the other hand, as His Word clearly states, He has also provided the means whereby His people can receive *divine* healing! God is the Author of both means of obtaining healing.

It's strange that we almost never question the doctor's word when he tells us to take a certain medication so we can get well. And we almost never question obtaining our healing by some other natural means such as improving our eating habits and getting the proper amount of rest each day. Most people will take a doctor's advice, or begin to improve their diet and get adequate sleep in order to recover from some ailment or to help themselves become well and strong. But when it comes to appropriating divine healing, they sometimes waver or question whether or not it will work for them! Natural means of obtaining healing are good and beneficial. But in some cases, there is only so much medical science can do; sometimes doctors have to tell their patients there's nothing more medical science can do for them. But, thank God, we know the Great Physician! He's our Healer and He will always heal us when we come to Him in faith according to His Word!

I'm not against hospitals or doctors. I thank God for what doctors and medical science can do to help suffering humanity. But I also thank God for divine healing because there are certain cases in the natural where medical doctors run into a dead-end street, so to speak. But with Jesus, our Great Physician, there are no dead-end streets! The Bible says, *"If thou canst believe, all things are possible to him that believeth"* (Mark 9:23).

We know from the Word that God is the Giver of every good gift. God not only provided divine healing for His people, but He has also provided natural means for man to be helped. We know that it is God who gives doctors and scientists the knowledge and the ability to develop medicine and medical procedures which save countless lives. We know *the devil* is certainly not helping man develop medicine that will help people and save lives, because that would be contrary to the Bible. The Bible says that the devil is our adversary or opponent and that he *"as a roaring lion, walketh about, seeking whom he may DEVOUR"* (1 Peter 5:8). John 10:10 also shows us what the devil is busy doing!

JOHN 10:10
10 The thief cometh not, but for TO STEAL, and TO KILL, and TO DESTROY: I [Jesus] am come that they might have life, and that they might have it more abundantly.

God has provided the avenue of medical science through which mankind can receive help and healing for the physical body. We know this because of James 1:17 which says that every good gift and every perfect gift is from God above; and doctors and medical science are certainly a benefit to mankind. So it is God who established the means whereby mankind can be helped through medical science.

Healing: God's Idea—Not Man's

Looking in the Old Testament, we also need to realize that it was *God's* idea, not man's, to establish a statute of divine healing for His people. It was then that God revealed Himself as our Physician—as Jehovah Rapha—*"The Lord that healeth."*

EXODUS 15:22–26

22 So Moses brought Israel from the Red sea, and they went out into the wilderness of Shur; and they went three days in the wilderness, and found no water.

23 And when they came to Marah, they could not drink of the waters of Marah, for they were bitter: therefore the name of it was called Marah.

24 And the people murmured against Moses, saying, What shall we drink?

25 And he cried unto the Lord; and the Lord shewed him a tree, which when he had cast into the waters, the waters were made sweet: there he made for them a statute and an ordinance, and there he proved them,

26 And said, If thou wilt diligently hearken to the voice of the Lord thy God . . . I will put [permit] none of these diseases upon thee, which I have brought upon the Egyptians: for I AM THE LORD THAT HEALETH THEE.

The Israelites were making their exodus out of Egypt where they had been in bondage and subject to the cruel slavery of Pharaoh and the Egyptians. They were on their way to the promised land, and on their journey they ventured into the wilderness of Shur and sojourned there for three days without any water. Then when they came to Marah and found water, they couldn't drink it because it was bitter. Moses cried to the Lord, and the Lord showed him a tree and told Moses to cast it into the water. When the tree was dipped into the water, the water became sweet so the children of Israel could drink it (Exod. 15:25).

The tree Moses cast into the waters is a semblance or a type of the tree that Jesus died on—the Cross of Calvary. In many places in the

Bible water is representative of *people*. Isn't it interesting that in the same way the tree was dipped into the waters at Marah and used to heal the waters, Jesus Christ, who died on a tree and rose again from the dead, was "dipped into the waters" of humanity, so to speak, to obtain our healing and our redemption!

EXODUS 15:26

26 If thou wilt diligently hearken to the voice of the Lord thy God, and wilt do that which is right in his sight, and wilt give ear to his commandments, and keep all his statutes, I will put [permit] none of these diseases upon thee, which I have brought upon the Egyptians: for I AM THE LORD THAT HEALETH THEE.

In Exodus 15:26, God established a statute of healing for His people. Nowhere in the Bible does it say that this statute of divine healing has been revoked, changed, or altered. In fact, Malachi 3:6 says, *"I am the Lord, I change not."* The Lord has never changed His mind or His will concerning the statute of divine healing. When God makes a covenant, or an agreement with His people, He abides by that covenant until it is revoked, stopped, or superseded by a better one. Therefore, since healing is also found in the New Testament, we know that God's healing covenant is still in force today. Besides that, because God established a statute of healing with His people the children of Israel—and the Bible says God never changes—we know that healing is still available for His people today. Actually, because of the redemptive work of Christ, the Bible says that we have a *better* covenant than the Israelites had, established upon *better* promises (Heb. 8:6)!

Your Part in Receiving Healing

"Yes, but I know someone who was prayed for and didn't get healed," you hear people say. But just because someone fails to receive healing doesn't mean the Word of God is false, or that God's covenant of healing is not in force today. I don't know why some people receive their healing and others do not. In some cases, we simply don't know everything there is to know. However, I do know that a person must mix *faith* with the Word in order to receive healing or any blessing or promise from God.

HEBREWS 4:2
2 **For unto us was the gospel preached, as well as unto them: but the word preached did not profit them, NOT BEING MIXED WITH FAITH in them that heard it.**

In other words, if we need healing, our faith has something to do with receiving healing from God because God's Word will always work when we act on it *in faith*. Just because someone failed to *receive* healing doesn't change the fact that healing belongs to us and that it's God's will that we walk in divine health.

Many times we don't understand why some good Christian people become sick and instead of receiving healing, they die and go on to be with the Lord. By the same token, we may not understand why everyone isn't saved either; but whether or not we understand why some people don't choose to accept their salvation, the Bible still teaches that salvation is available to all. We may not understand why things happen as they do, but a lack of understanding on our part does not discredit the Word of God. The Word says, "Believe you receive and you SHALL HAVE" (Mark 11:24).

From time to time, there may be people whom I lay hands upon to be healed, who fail to receive their healing. But I'm not going to quit laying hands on people and praying for their healing because some fail to receive healing. I'm going to keep on laying hands on the sick because *the Bible* says believers are to lay hands on the sick and they will recover (Mark 16:18), and because God has anointed me to minister to the sick.

Chapter 3

Healing in the
Church Today

There is evidence throughout the pages of God's Word that healing belongs to us as believers today. In Deuteronomy chapter 28, for
instance, both the blessings for keeping God's laws and the curses
for breaking God's laws are listed. Verse 61 lists the consequences
for breaking the Law. It says, *"Also EVERY SICKNESS, and EVERY
PLAGUE, which is not written in the book of this law, them will the
Lord bring upon thee, until thou be destroyed."* Galatians 3:13 states
our rights and privileges in Christ which include redemption from the
curse of the Law: *"Christ hath REDEEMED US from the curse of the
law, being made a curse for us."* Since *every* sickness and *every* plague was
included in the curse of the Law then Christ has paid the price for *every
sickness* and *every plague* for us in our redemption! *". . . who healeth ALL
thy diseases"* (Ps. 103:3)!

What Do *You* Believe?

Spiritually, there are basically three classes or categories of people
in the world today. One, there are those who altogether reject the blood
of Jesus Christ as the only means for remission of sin. Two, there are
those who accept the blood of Jesus for the remission of sin *only*, but
deny that the redemptive work of Christ includes healing of sickness
and disease. In other words, these people stop at *"Who forgiveth all
thine iniquities . . ."* (Ps. 103:3). They overlook the last part of that verse
which says, *"who HEALETH all thy DISEASES"*! They have a problem
seeing Jesus as the Healer of diseases. He is their Savior, all right, but

either they haven't been taught correctly or they just don't believe the healing aspect of our redemption.

Then, three, there are those who accept the Bible as the inspired Word of God and believe Jesus is the Redeemer from sin *and* from sickness and disease. These people believe that our redemption includes God's blessings—salvation, healing from sickness and disease, protection, and abundant life—and that we are to enjoy these provisions while we're here on the earth!

Receive Healing by Faith

The Bible is very explicit about the benefits of redemption including healing of sickness and disease as well as remission and forgiveness of sin. But if one of the benefits of our redemption belongs to us today, then *all* of the benefits of redemption belong to us today. There are some Christians who go through the Bible and pick out portions of Scripture, and say, "This is God's will for us!" However, then they choose other portions of Scripture and say in effect, "This is not for everyone," or "This is not God's will for us today." If they're going to do that, they might as well throw the whole Bible away, because if part of it isn't true, then all of it is a farce! But, thank God, the whole Bible is true! Healing is for everyone because God is no respecter of persons. What He has done for someone else, He'll do for *you!* And we can be assured that it's God's will to heal people *today* because, *"Jesus Christ* [is] *the same yesterday, and to day, and for ever"* (Heb. 13:8)! Divine healing is available to us today!

We've seen healing in the statute of healing God established for His people in Exodus 15:26 for keeping His law or obeying His Word. We've also seen healing in the benefits of redemption that God has provided for His people. We know that God never changes and that Jesus is the same yesterday, today, and forever (Mal. 3:6; Heb. 13:8). Therefore, we need to realize that healing is as much ours today as it was for the children of Israel in the Old Testament. Healing is as much ours today as it was for those who lived in New Testament times when Jesus walked upon the earth. And healing is as much ours today as it was for the Early Church.

However, it's up to us whether or not we *receive* by faith those things which belong to us in Christ. It's when we continually confess God's Word and believe we receive the blessings we need, that "the switch of faith" is turned on and God's power is released in our own lives. God will make His Word good in our lives if we will believe it and act upon it!

Healing in the Ministry of Jesus

Jesus is our Example. Therefore, since Jesus believed in and preached that healing is God's will for us, we should believe and preach the same thing. We see healing demonstrated in the ministry of Jesus while He was on the earth. In fact, looking at the life of Jesus in the four Gospels, you will notice that one of the most distinguishing features of Jesus' ministry was His *healing* ministry. Yes, Jesus' teaching ministry was also one of the most *significant* aspects of His earthly ministry, because He had to continually teach the people to get them to a place of faith so they could receive their healing. We know that faith comes by hearing and hearing by the Word of God, and Jesus taught the people the Word; He proclaimed the gospel message as He went from place to place teaching the people (Rom. 10:17).

LUKE 4:18

18 **The Spirit of the Lord is upon me, because he hath anointed me to preach the gospel to the poor; he hath sent me TO HEAL the brokenhearted, to preach DELIVERANCE to the captives, and RECOVERING OF SIGHT to the blind, TO SET AT LIBERTY them that are bruised.**

Not only did Jesus teach, but the Bible also says the Spirit of the Lord was upon Jesus to *preach* the gospel. Luke 4:18 is the message that Jesus proclaimed to the people as He went into the synagogues to teach and to preach. Teaching and preaching the gospel included teaching and preaching about divine healing as we can see in Luke 4:18, because the gospel message is also a *healing message.*

Another reason healing was one of the most distinguishing features of Jesus' ministry is because Jesus *demonstrated* what He preached and taught with signs following. Yes, there were other teachers in Jesus' day. For example, the rabbis were those we would call the doctors of the Jewish law—very learned men in all aspects of Jewish law—and they taught in the synagogues too. But what distinguished Jesus from all other teachers was the *power* and *demonstration* of the Holy Spirit in His ministry. The Bible says Jesus, *"went about all Galilee, TEACHING in their synagogues, and PREACHING the gospel of the kingdom, and HEALING ALL MANNER OF SICKNESS and ALL MANNER OF DISEASE among the people"* (Matt. 4:23). There were distinctive, supernatural signs which included healing and miracles following Jesus' ministry as He proclaimed God's Word.

However, even though everywhere Jesus went He proclaimed, "The Spirit of the Lord is upon Me to heal," there were some people who rejected His message. For example, when Jesus healed the paralytic man who was lowered through the ceiling by four others, the Bible says, *". . . the power of the Lord was present to heal them* [all]*"* (Luke 5:17). In other words, the healing power was in manifestation to heal *every single person* in that house, but only one paralytic man received his healing by faith!

Even John the Baptist, the one who was the forerunner to Jesus' ministry, came to a point in his life when he wondered, and doubted if Jesus was really the long-awaited Christ. If you'll remember, when Jesus came to be baptized by John in the Jordan River, John himself had said, *"I have need to be baptized OF THEE, and comest thou to ME?"* (Matt. 3:14). And then the Holy Spirit descended from heaven in bodily shape like a dove and lighted upon Jesus. A Voice came from heaven saying, *"This is my beloved Son, in whom I am well pleased"* (Matt. 3:16–17). In other words, John knew and openly declared that Jesus was the Christ. And John was also the one who had previously said, *"One mightier than I cometh, the latchet of whose shoes I am not worthy to unloose"* (Luke 3:16).

However, when John was later imprisoned by Herod, he sent two of his disciples to ask Jesus, *"Art thou he that should come, or do we look for another?"* (Matt. 11:3). Doubt is one of the greatest enemies to faith.

Notice how Jesus answered John's disciples when they questioned Him, asking, "Are You the Christ?" Jesus cited His healing ministry as one proof that He was the Messiah.

MATTHEW 11:4–5

4 . . . Go and shew John again those things which ye do hear and see:

5 The blind receive their sight, and the lame walk, the lepers are cleansed, and the deaf hear, the dead are raised up, and the poor have the gospel preached to them.

John needed to be encouraged in His faith in Jesus as the Messiah; his faith needed to be rekindled, so to speak. So in order to encourage John, Jesus merely gave John's disciples the evidence of the miraculous signs and wonders that followed His ministry as proof that He was and is the Messiah. The Bible says, *"faith cometh by hearing, and hearing by the word of God"* (Rom 10:17), so that's why Jesus sent word to John: The blind see, the lame walk, the lepers are cleansed, the deaf hear, the dead are raised, and the poor have the gospel preached to them!

Healing is one of the signs that follow the preaching of the gospel. In His earthly ministry Jesus preached the gospel; therefore, it's no wonder that mighty signs, wonders, and miracles followed His ministry.

The Bible teaches that the preaching of the gospel will bring the power of God into manifestation, and the healing anointing will be present to heal. We can see that Jesus operated in a strong healing anointing in His earthly ministry because He went from village to village proclaiming the gospel and as a result the power of God was continually in manifestation.

ACTS 10:38

38 How God anointed Jesus of Nazareth with the Holy Ghost and with power: who went about doing good, and HEALING ALL THAT WERE OPPRESSED OF THE DEVIL; for God was with him.

Acts 10:38 raises the question in some people's minds, *Does that mean everyone who is suffering with sickness or disease has a demon or an evil spirit in them?* No. Just because someone is sick doesn't mean an evil spirit is present in his or her body. There *can be* an evil spirit oppressing a person and enforcing the sickness or disease, but that is not necessarily so in every case. However, we do know that everything that's bad comes from the enemy and everything that's good comes from God. We know that because the Bible says, *"The thief cometh not, but for to steal and to kill and to destroy: I* [Jesus] *am come that they might have life, and that they might have it more abundantly"* (John 10:10).

Jesus Christ the Eternal Cure

Not only did Jesus have a healing anointing in His earthly ministry, but He also bore our sicknesses and diseases on the Cross. The prophet Isaiah foretold this more than seven hundred years before Christ came to the earth as a man. He prophesied that Jesus would not only bear our sins but that He would bear our sicknesses and diseases on the Cross (Isa. 53:4–5). Jesus fulfilled that prophecy in His death, burial, and resurrection. And as we will see, in the Book of Acts we find that the apostles got ahold of that revelation and went out in the Name of Jesus healing the sick. Peter had so much of the power of God flowing through him that as he walked down the street and his shadow fell upon people, they were healed (Acts 5:15)!

Divine Healing in the Ministry of the Disciples

We've looked at healing in the Old Testament and we've seen divine healing in God's plan of redemption. Then we've seen that Jesus, our Example, ministered divine healing in His earthly ministry. Now let's look at divine healing in the ministry of the apostles and the disciples. We will also see that Jesus commissioned the Church to minister divine healing to the sick in His Name.

MATTHEW 10:1
1 **And when he** [Jesus] **had called unto him his twelve disciples, he gave them power against unclean spirits, to cast them out, and to heal all manner of sickness and all manner of disease.**

MARK 6:12–13
12 **And they** [Jesus' disciples] **went out, and preached that men should repent.**
13 **And they cast out many devils, and anointed with oil many that were sick, and healed them.**

ACTS 5:12
12 **And by the hands of the apostles were many signs snd wonders wrought among the people. . . .**

ACTS 2:43
43 **And fear came upon every soul: and many wonders and signs were done by the apostles.**

The disciples were able to minister the healing power of God because they were filled with the Holy Spirit. We read in Acts 2:4 that on the day of Pentecost the disciples and many others were filled with the Holy Spirit and began to speak with other tongues as the Holy Spirit gave them utterance. The disciples and those gathered with them were endued with power from on High as they were assembled together in that upper room. Peter and John were included in that assembly. Let's look at some of the effects of being endued with power from on High in the lives of Peter and John.

ACTS 3:1–8

1 Now Peter and John went up together into the temple at the hour of prayer, being the ninth hour.

2 And a certain man lame from his mother's womb was carried, whom they laid daily at the gate of the temple which is called Beautiful, to ask alms of them that entered into the temple;

3 Who seeing Peter and John about to go into the temple asked an alms.

4 And Peter, fastening his eyes upon him with John, said, Look on us.

5 And he gave heed unto them, expecting to receive something of them.

6 Then Peter said, Silver and gold have I none; but such as I have give I thee: IN THE NAME OF JESUS CHRIST OF NAZARETH RISE UP AND WALK.

7 And he took him by the right hand, and lifted him up: and immediately his feet and ankle bones received strength.

8 And he leaping up stood, and walked, and entered with them into the temple, walking, and leaping, and praising God.

The Name of Jesus, spoken through the disciples' lips, healed a poor crippled man! Healings were wrought by the disciples in the Name of Jesus because Jesus Himself had given the disciples the power or the authority to heal the sick in His Name.

MATTHEW 10:1

1 And when he [Jesus] had called unto him his twelve disciples, he gave them power against unclean spirits, to cast them out, and to heal all manner of sickness and all manner of disease.

Notice it says that Jesus gave the disciples power to heal *all manner* of sickness and *all manner* of disease. All manner of sickness and disease includes every minor ailment that can be named as well as every major illness or disease—including terminal diseases.

Someone might say, "Yes, but that was just the twelve disciples. *They* were especially anointed by Jesus. Of course, *they* could heal all manner of sickness and disease." But the healing anointing was not given exclusively to the twelve alone. For example, in Luke chapter 10, Jesus commissioned seventy other disciples and gave them instructions to heal the sick as He sent them into cities two by two. And we will also see that Jesus commissioned or authorized the Church of the Lord Jesus Christ—*all believers*—to heal the sick.

LUKE 10:1, 8–9

1 . . . the Lord appointed other seventy also, and sent them two and two before his face into every city and place, wither he himself would come. . . .

8 [Jesus said unto the seventy disciples] And into whatsoever city ye enter, and they receive you, eat such things as are set before you:

9 And HEAL THE SICK that are therein, and say unto them, The kingdom of God is come nigh unto you.

Then in Mark chapter 16, Jesus issued the Great Commission to the Church—to the whole Body of Christ—past, present, and future. The Great Commission includes healing the sick by the authority of the Name of Jesus.

MARK 16:15–18

15 Go ye into all the world, and preach the gospel to every creature.

16 He that believeth and is baptized shall be saved; but he that believeth not shall be damned.

17 And THESE SIGNS SHALL FOLLOW THEM THAT BELIEVE; in my name shall they cast out devils; they shall speak with new tongues;

18 They shall take up serpents; and if they drink any deadly thing, it shall not hurt them; THEY SHALL LAY HANDS ON THE SICK, and THEY SHALL RECOVER.

From the Book of Acts, we see that healing and miracles were an integral part of the ministry of the Early Church. The Apostle Paul, a powerful leader in the Early Church, stated in Romans 15:19, *"Through mighty signs and wonders, by the power of the Spirit of God. . . I have fully preached the gospel of Christ."* Healing and miracles follow the preaching of the gospel, and as the Church of the Lord Jesus Christ is faithful to preach the Word, signs and wonders will follow!

From the Book of Acts through the Epistles and then throughout church history, we can see that healing has always been a distinct characteristic of the Church of the Lord Jesus Christ. Jesus said, *"He that believeth on me, the works that I do shall he do also; and greater works than these shall he do; because I go unto my Father"* (John 14:12).

—Chapter 4—

Divine Healing Is Available to God's People Today

We've looked at the statute of divine healing that God established for His people in Exodus 15:26. Then we saw healing in the plan of redemption: *"Who his own self bare our sins in his own body on the tree, that we, being dead to sins, should live unto righteousness: by whose stripes ye were healed"* (1 Peter 2:24). We saw the healing power of God in Jesus' earthly ministry, and we saw that Jesus commissioned the disciples and then the Church to preach the gospel and to heal the sick.

Healing is as much ours today as it was for the children of Israel in the Old Testament. Healing is as much ours today as it was for those who lived when Jesus walked upon the earth. And healing is as much ours today as it was for the Early Church. We know this because the Bible says, *"I am the Lord, I change not"* (Mal. 3:6). And Hebrews 13:8 says, *"Jesus Christ the same yesterday, and to day, and for ever."* God's will concerning healing is the same for the Church today as it has always been for His people. The healing that Jesus purchased for each one of us in His death, burial, and resurrection is available to all today.

One argument we hear against healing being for us today comes from many modern-day theologians who say that miracles and healings passed away when the last of the twelve apostles died. One reason this couldn't be true is that in the Bible there were more than just twelve apostles! Certainly the Book of Revelation talks about the twelve apostles of the Lamb; that is, the original twelve who followed Jesus in His earth walk. But we already read in Luke 10:1 that Jesus

27

anointed seventy other disciples besides the twelve to go out and do the work of the ministry. Barnabas and Paul were two more apostles who ministered God's healing power, and they were not included with the original twelve apostles who followed Jesus in His earthly ministry. We know that healing was characteristic of the Apostle Paul's ministry because the Bible says that mighty signs and wonders followed as Paul preached the gospel (Rom. 15:19). Besides that, as we've already seen, the Lord Jesus Christ commissioned *all believers* to preach the gospel and to heal the sick (Mark 16:15–18)! If you are a Christian, then *"all believers"* includes you! *You* have been commissioned or authorized by Jesus Christ the Head of the Church to preach the gospel and to heal the sick.

Divine Healing in the History of the Church

If healing stopped with the last of the apostles as some people say, then why do we have documented historical records of divine healings that date *after* the death of the apostles? For instance, in A.D. 165, Justin Martyr, an Early Church father, made the following statement about divine healing:

> For numberless demoniacs throughout the whole world, and in your city, many of our Christian men exorcising them in the name of Jesus Christ, who was crucified under Pontius Pilate, HAVE HEALED and DO HEAL, rendering helpless and driving the possessing devils out of the men, though they could not be cured by all the other exorcists, and those who used incantations and drugs. (*The Second Apology of Justin*, Chapter 6)

In A.D. 200, another Early Church father, Irenaeus, also declared that the Church has authority to heal the sick in Jesus' Name:

> . . . those who are in truth His disciples, receiving grace from Him, do in His name perform [miracles], so as to promote the welfare of other men. . . . For some do certainly and truly drive out devils . . . Others still, HEAL THE SICK by laying their hands upon them, and THEY ARE MADE WHOLE. Yea,

moreover, as I have said, the dead even have been raised up, and remained among us for many years. (*Irenaeus Against Heresies*, Book I, Chapter 32, Section 4)

Irenaeus was a pupil of Polycarp who according to historical records, was a disciple of the Apostle John. Justin Martyr and Irenaeus penned these words more than 150 years after Christ had ascended to the right hand of God! Yet, many modern-day theologians say healing passed away after the death of the last apostle! But, you see, the Church of the Lord Jesus Christ had the same authority to heal the sick in the time of Justin Martyr and Irenaeus as it did in the Book of Acts, *and* as it does today. Healing the sick has always been a characteristic of the Church of the Lord Jesus Christ.

In A.D. 250, a Christian scholar and an Early Church father by the name of Origen wrote about Christians healing the sick in his day:

And some give evidence of their having received through this faith a marvellous power BY THE CURES which they perform, invoking no other name over those who need their help than that of the God of all things, and of Jesus, along with a mention of His history. For by these means we too have seen many persons FREED FROM GRIEVOUS CALAMITIES, and from DISTRACTIONS OF MIND, AND MADNESS, and COUNTLESS OTHER ILLS, which could be cured neither by men nor devils. (*Origen Against Celsus*, Book III, Chapter 24)

The Bible says, *"For this purpose the Son of God was manifested, THAT HE MIGHT DESTROY THE WORKS OF THE DEVIL"* (1 John 3:8). What are the works of the devil? We know that all sin is the work of the enemy, Satan. But the Bible also says that *sickness and disease* are works of the enemy.

ACTS 10:38
38 How God anointed Jesus of Nazareth with the Holy Ghost and with power: who went about doing good, and HEALING ALL THAT WERE OPPRESSED OF THE DEVIL; for God was with him.

In the writings of Clement, a noted theologian living in the third century and a proponent of divine healing, we can see that Clement also believed as the Bible teaches that sick people should be healed of their afflictions.

> . . . he [Clement] ordered those to approach who were distressed with diseases; and thus many approached, having come together through the experience of those who had been healed yesterday. And he having laid his hands upon them and prayed, and immediately healed them. . . . (*The Homilies of Clement*, Homily IX, Chapter 23)

Gregory of Nazianzus was a fourth-century bishop who presided over the church in Constantinople. The church historian Sozomen attested to the manifestations of the power of God which occurred in Gregory's church.

> . . . the power of God was there manifested, and was helpful both in waking visions and in dreams, often for the relief of many diseases and for those afflicted by some sudden transmutation in their affairs. (*The Ecclesiastical History of Sozomen*, Chapter 5)

Citing one such example, Bozomen gave this account of the healing of a pregnant woman who had died due to an accident:

> . . . one day, when the people were met together for worship in this edifice, a pregnant woman fell from the highest gallery, and was found dead on the spot; but that, at the prayer of the whole congregation, SHE WAS RESTORED TO LIFE, AND SHE AND THE INFANT WERE SAVED. (*Ibid.*, Chapter 5)

Does this sound like healing passed away after the twelve apostles died? No, throughout history we have documented evidence of healings and miracles performed in the Name of Jesus. Augustine, a great Christian scholar and bishop of Hippo from A.D. 396 to 430, reported many healings which were wrought in his day by the Name of Jesus. In approximately A.D. 424, Augustine wrote the following account attesting to miracles that were performed through the mighty Name of Jesus:

> FOR EVEN NOW miracles are wrought in the name of Jesus Christ . . . once I realized how many miracles were occurring in our own day and which were so like the miracles of old and also how wrong it would be to allow the memory of these marvels of divine power to perish from among our people. It is only two years ago that the keeping of records was begun here in Hippo, and already, at this writing, we have nearly seventy attested miracles. (*The City of God*, Book XXII, Chapter 8)[1]

In fact, until the close of the sixth century, Christians widely adhered to the message of divine healing as it is taught in the Scriptures. In other words, the Christian population generally believed that healing was *always* God's will and that sickness and disease were satanic oppression and should be cured in every case by means of prayer and by invoking the Name of Jesus. However, with the advent of the reign of Pope Gregory I in A.D. 590, the pure message of divine healing began to be obscured by Gregory's belief that sickness and disease were one of the ways God chastised His children. Gregory saw sickness as the scourge of God's discipline and wrath instead of the result of satanic oppression. As his thinking gained popularity, sickness was no longer widely regarded as the work of the enemy, nor was it any longer thought that the sick should be healed in every instance.

Despite Gregory's influence on the church at Rome, Christians never questioned God's *power or ability* to heal. However, more and more Christians did begin to question God's *willingness* to heal. During this time, the impact of this pervading thought seemed to put a damper on the supernatural manifestation of God's power in the Church as a whole until the Reformation in the sixteenth century.

With the Reformation came the rediscovery and the recovery of the truth of the doctrine of grace and the more widespread acceptance of the Scriptures as a basis for church doctrine and practices. Martin Luther, formerly an Augustinian monk, was the foremost leader of the

Reformation and the founder of the Protestant church. Luther believed in divine healing and ministered to the sick based on the authority of the Scriptures.

One well-known incident which occurred in Luther's ministry was the healing of his friend, Philip Melancthon, who was a noted scholar of the Reformation. Finding his friend near death due to a sickness, history reports that upon visiting Melancthon, Luther went to a window in his friend's room and prayed fervently to God. Then he went to the sickbed where Melancthon lay, took him by the hand and said: "Be of good courage, Philip, you will not die; give no place to the spirit of sorrow, and be not your own murderer, but trust in the Lord. . . ."[2] After that, Melancthon immediately became cheerful and began to improve. He regained his health and strength completely.

Moving even closer to our day, another religious reformer and revivalist named Zinzendorf who lived in the 1700's, also testified of the many healings which were wrought by the Name of Jesus in his lifetime. Zinzendorf wrote the following account of instances of divine healing in his day:

> To believe against hope is the root of the gift of miracles; and I owe this testimony to our beloved church, that APOSTOLIC POWERS ARE THERE MANIFESTED. WE HAVE HAD UNDENIABLE PROOFS thereof in the unequivocal discovery of things, persons, and circumstances, which could not humanly have been discovered, IN THE HEALING OF MALADIES IN THEMSELVES INCURABLE, SUCH AS CANCERS, CONSUMPTIONS, when THE PATIENT WAS IN THE AGONIES OF DEATH, all by means of prayer, or of a single word.[3]

If you'll study church history, you'll find that the patriarchs of our Christian heritage and those who were involved in the great moves of God through the years, played a vital role in carrying the anointing of God and the revelation from God's Word about healing to their generation. They faced many obstacles and challenges to their faith to do so, but God has always had a people whom He has used to lift high the blood-stained banner of Jesus Christ and to declare the truth of the gospel of Jesus Christ—which includes healing!

Another group of revivalists, the Waldensians, writing as late as 1750, also substantiated that divine healing is a present-tense fact and is available to Christians everywhere:

> Therefore, concerning the anointing of the sick, we hold it as an article of faith, and profess sincerely from the heart, THAT SICK PERSONS, WHEN THEY ASK IT, MAY LAWFULLY BE ANOINTED WITH ANOINTING OIL BY ONE WHO JOINS WITH THEM IN PRAYING THAT IT MAY BE EFFICACIOUS TO THE HEALING OF THE BODY according to the design and end and effect mentioned by the apostles, and we profess that such an anointing, performed according to the apostolic design and practice, will be healing and profitable.[4]

The brightly burning torch of divine healing which had been progressively carried through the centuries by men and women of God, was then passed into the hand of the Oxford-trained orator, John Wesley, in the mid-1700's. Wesley, an English theologian, evangelist, and founder of the Methodist church, cited in his journal many instances of divine healings which occurred in his own ministry, including a rather interesting entry detailing the healing of his lame horse!

> When Mr. Shepherd and I left Smeton, my horse was so exceeding lame that I was afraid I must have lain by too. We could not discern what it was that was amiss; and yet he would scarce set his foot to the ground. By riding thus seven miles, I was thoroughly tired, and my head ached more than it had done for some months. . . . I then thought, "Cannot God heal either man or beast, by any means, or without any?" Immediately my weariness and headache ceased, and my horse's lameness in the same instant. Nor did he halt any more either that day or the next. . . . (Monday, March 17, 1746)[5]

This revival of healing that came about with the Reformation did not remain on the European continent, but quickly spread to the American frontier. From European revivalists to the ministers of the American frontier such as Peter Cartwright the famous circuit-riding preacher, and of course many others, the message of God's love and compassion for mankind and His healing power began to span much of the then-known American continent. Throughout history we see that everywhere the people of God have embraced the Spirit of truth and wherever the full gospel of Jesus Christ has been preached, there has always been the demonstration of the Holy Spirit with signs following—including the power to heal and to deliver mankind. So many are the recorded instances of miracles of divine healings throughout church history, that time and space would fail to tell of them all.

Entering the period of the late nineteenth and early twentieth centuries, proponents of the message of divine healing continued to carry the torch of God's healing power to the sick and the afflicted. Some of these early pioneers and advocates of divine healing include such notable persons as: A. J. Gordon, A. B. Simpson, John Alexander Dowie, John G. Lake, Aimee Semple McPherson, Smith Wigglesworth, the Jeffreys brothers—Stephen and George, and Charles Price, to name just a few.

I grew up during the great twentieth century healing revival which lasted from 1947 through 1958, and I often helped my father, Rev. Kenneth E. Hagin, with his meetings which sometimes continued as long as nine weeks at a time. During this revival of divine healing, the organization known as "The Voice of Healing" began. Serving as a forum for the propagation of the gospel message of healing to the world, "The Voice of Healing" attracted well over one hundred members, some of which included: Gordon Lindsay, Velmer Gardner, Raymond T. Richey, Jack Coe, T. L. Osborn, and my dad, Kenneth E. Hagin. These evangelists proclaimed Jesus as the Healer of sickness and disease *today*, and the reality of divine healing was made apparent by the miraculous signs and wonders which were commonly demon-strated in their ministries.

In every age and in every dispensation—past, present, and future—the supernatural power of God has always been and will always be in operation where the gospel is preached, to deliver God's people and to bless humanity! We have seen healing evidenced in the Old Testament, in Jesus' earthly ministry, in the Early Church, and *throughout Church history.* As I said previously, nowhere do we find the slightest hint or suggestion that God has changed His mind regarding the subject of divine healing!

Experiencing Divine Healing for Yourself

Also, just speaking practically, there is much personal testimony as to the reality of divine healing being available to God's people today. For example, from the time I was a child, I myself have witnessed the healing power of God in manifestation. When I was about two years old, I began sitting on the platform as my dad, Kenneth E. Hagin, preached the gospel. I have seen people get up out of wheelchairs perfectly healed. I have seen people with all kinds of maladies and diseases become well and whole again by the power of God. Some of them were healed instantly, and some of them began to gradually amend from the time hands were laid upon them in faith. Others were healed "as they went" in faith, which is entirely biblical according to Luke 17:14.

LUKE 17:11–14

11 And it came to pass, as he [Jesus] went to Jerusalem, that he passed through the midst of Samaria and Galilee.

12 And as he entered into a certain village, there met him ten men that were lepers, which stood afar off:

13 And they lifted up their voices, and said, Jesus, Master, have mercy on us.

14 And when he saw them, he said unto them, Go shew yourselves unto the priests. And it came to pass, that, AS THEY WENT, THEY WERE CLEANSED.

I personally have seen the healing power of God in manifestation many, many times. Therefore, people who don't believe in divine healing have come too late to tell me that healing is not real and that it's not for us today!

If you've ever experienced divine healing, I guarantee you there's no theologian or anyone *anywhere* who can convince you that healing is not real. This is especially true if you've been healed of an incurable illness or of a terminal disease. No one would be able to convince a person who has experienced divine healing that healing isn't real! For example, I once heard a man say, "The baptism in the Holy Spirit is not real." Another replied, "Have you *experienced* the baptism in the Holy Spirit?" "Well, no," he admitted. The other man responded, "Well, I *have*, and you've come too late to tell me it's not real!" It's the same way with healing!

When I was about three years old, my dad was pastoring a church in Farmersville, Texas. He'd preach specifically on the subject of healing on Saturday nights and people would come from all the surrounding towns and communities to be in those meetings.

Farmersville was a farming town, and back in those days everyone came to town on Saturday night to go to the public theater or just to visit with one another in the town square. There wasn't anywhere else to go for entertainment and very few people had television sets in those days.

Dad held healing services in that town every Saturday night. Someone once said to him, "Preacher, you've got more people at this church on Saturday nights than there are at the town square and in the picture show put together!" The healing power of God is what drew the crowds!

Then I remember when Dad began ministering on the road. Mom, my sister Pat, and I would travel with him from time to time. On those occasions when I did travel with my dad, I would stay up as late as he did after meetings as he and mom would visit with other ministers. I didn't want to miss anything, so I would listen closely as they talked about the move of God and the healing power of God. As I mentioned previously, over the years I saw many people healed in my dad's ministry.

God's Compassion Demonstrated in Healing

Therefore, I grew up understanding the compassion of God and God's willingness to heal and deliver the afflicted, and I witnessed the healing power of God with my own eyes! Through the years, my favorite illustration in the Bible about healing is found in the account of blind Bartimaeus. It made such an impression on me as a child growing up because it showed God's compassion and willingness to heal.

MARK 10:46–52

46 And they came to Jericho: and as he [Jesus] went out of Jericho with his disciples and a great number of people, blind Bartimaeus, the son of Timaeus, sat by the highway side begging.

47 And when he heard that it was Jesus of Nazareth, he began to cry out, and say, Jesus, thou son of David, have mercy on me.

48 And many charged him that he should hold his peace: but he cried the more a great deal, Thou son of David, have mercy on me.

49 And Jesus stood still, and commanded him to be called. And they call the blind man, saying unto him, Be of good comfort, rise; he calleth thee.

50 And he, casting away his garment, rose, and came to Jesus.

51 And Jesus answered and said unto him, What wilt thou that I should do unto thee? The blind man said unto him, Lord, that I might receive my sight.

52 And Jesus said unto him, Go thy way; thy faith hath made thee whole. And immediately he received his sight, and followed Jesus in the way.

As blind Bartimaeus sat by the wayside on the Jericho road, he heard a commotion as Jesus and the crowds were approaching. Bartimaeus probably asked someone nearby, "Hey, what's going on?" "Jesus of Nazareth is passing by," someone out of the crowd probably responded. When blind Bartimaeus discovered it was Jesus who was approaching, he began to cry out, "Jesus, Son of David! Have mercy on me!"

But the religious people who were crowded around Bartimaeus tried to squelch his faith. They may have told him to sit down and be quiet. That sounds like something religious people might say today. But if you don't go to Jesus with your need, He can't come to you! You see, Jesus through His death, burial, and resurrection has already come to people everywhere to save, heal, and deliver them. But they must *receive* that by faith—they must receive the salvation God so freely offers them. Then as believers, Christians must go to God in faith and appropriate what already belongs to them.

Bartimaeus did that. Healing belonged to him, and he received it by faith. As Jesus was passing by, blind Bartimaeus would not have received anything from Jesus if he hadn't insisted on being heard. But as it happened, the more the people told Bartimaeus to be quiet, the louder he screamed, and Jesus Christ, because of His great compassion and His willingness to heal mankind, stopped and listened at the sound of Bartimaeus' cry. Turning to Bartimaeus, Jesus gave Bartimaeus His full attention and asked him, "What do you want?"

According to tradition, people of different classes or strata of society in that day wore different types of garments to represent their status in life. It's been reported that Bartimaeus wore a certain type of cloak which identified him as a blind man and a beggar. The Bible says that when Jesus called for blind Bartimaeus, Bartimaeus threw his cloak aside and went to Jesus. In other words, the minute Jesus called for him, Bartimaeus stopped identifying with the past; he stopped seeing himself as a blind beggar and began to see himself well and whole!

MARK 10:49–50

49 And Jesus stood still, and commanded him to be called. And they call the blind man, saying unto him, Be of good comfort, rise; he calleth thee.

50 And he, CASTING AWAY HIS GARMENT, rose, and came to Jesus.

Casting away his garment was Bartimaeus' act of faith that he would receive his healing. In other words, from the minute Jesus called for him, Bartimaeus envisioned himself with his need met. He knew he wouldn't need that cloak anymore identifying him as a blind man and a beggar, so he threw it off his shoulders and eagerly went to meet Jesus. Jesus asked him, "What do you want?" Bartimaeus answered, "I want to see!" Jesus said, *"Go thy way; thy faith hath made thee whole."* (Mark 10:52). And Bartimaeus received his sight!

Notice there was no hesitation in Jesus' response to Bartimaeus' desperate cry to be healed! Jesus said, "Go your way; your faith has made you whole!" And Jesus Christ is the same yesterday, today, and forever! That same Jesus can still hear the cry of faith today! And Jesus is still asking, "What do you want Me to do for you?" Be specific with God as you make your requests known to Him. If you need healing, you know from the Word of God that healing is the will of God for you and that it has been provided for you in Christ. *Healing belongs to you.* It's already yours now. That's a Bible fact! As we've seen, even history itself confirms the reality of healing as God's will for us today.

If you are born again, it's up to you to receive what rightfully belongs to you. Only you can appropriate or receive for yourself what has already been so freely provided in redemption. God is waiting for you to appropriate healing or whatever it is you need from Him by faith. We find that principle stated in Mark 11:23–24.

MARK 11:23–24

23 For verily I say unto you, That whosoever shall say unto this mountain, Be thou removed, and be thou cast into the sea; and shall not

doubt in his heart, but shall believe that those things which he saith
shall come to pass; he shall have whatsoever he saith.

24 Therefore I say unto you, What things soever ye desire, when ye pray,
BELIEVE THAT YE RECEIVE THEM, and YE SHALL HAVE
THEM.

In other words, if you believe you receive healing, you shall have healing. Or we could say it like this: He who believes, *has*.

If you have not been able to receive your healing in the past for whatever reason, come to God with an honest and sincere heart. Look to God's Word, and rely on His promise to heal you. Then appropriate what rightfully belongs to you in the redemption God has so graciously provided for you through Jesus Christ.

If you have perhaps doubted God's Word, and have doubted that it is God's will for you to be well and victorious in life, ask God to forgive you. Maybe you haven't understood until now that it is God's will to heal you and make you whole. But if you'll look to God and search His Word, God will establish this powerful truth in your heart!

God is still in the business of healing people today! It doesn't matter how many times we've heard it—we need to continually hear and be reminded of God's Word—that it is God's will for us to be well and healthy and to enjoy the benefits of our redemption in this life. I like the saying, "It's God's will that we have some of heaven *to go to heaven in!*" God's statute of divine healing is in force today because the Bible says God never changes. We have an everlasting covenant with God for healing in the redemption provided through the shed blood of the Lord Jesus Christ.

Once you understand that healing is God's will for you and that God has provided healing for you in His great plan of redemption, then all you need to do is receive what already belongs to you by faith. Whether you receive healing through the laying on of hands, by the anointing with oil, or by simply hearing the Word of God and receiving healing on your own, it is important to remember to "keep the switch of faith turned on." In other words, take God at His Word and keep affirming that you believe Him and His Word. Keep affirming, "The healing power of God is working in my body to effect a healing and a cure." As you continue to believe God—that His Word is true and that the healing anointing is working on your behalf—healing will come!

We can take God at His Word, believe it, and receive His promises as ours. We can be fully persuaded, and have an unshakable faith in God that what He has promised, He is able also to perform, because healing is forever settled!

---

[1] Morton T. Kelsey, *Healing and Christianity in Ancient Thought and Modern Times* (New York: Harper and Row, 1973), p. 185.

[2] Carl J. Scherzer, *The Church and Healing* (Philadelphia: The Westminster Press, 1950), p.67.

[3] Dr. T. J. McCrossan, *Bodily Healing and the Atonement*, ed. Roy H. Hicks and Kenneth E. Hagin (Tulsa, Oklahoma: Kenneth Hagin Ministries, 1982), p. 54–55.

[4] McCrossan, p. 55.

[5] John Wesley, *The Journal of John Wesley*, ed. Percy Livingstone Parker (Chicago: Moody Press, 1974), p. 146.

Rhema Word Partner Club

WORKING *together* TO REACH THE WORLD!

People. Power. Purpose.

Have you ever dropped a stone into water? Small waves rise up at the point of impact and travel in all directions. It's called a ripple effect. That's the kind of impact Christians are meant to have in this world—the kind of impact that the Rhema family is producing in the earth today.

The Rhema Word Partner Club links Christians with a shared interest in reaching people with the Gospel and the message of faith in God.

Together we are reaching across generations, cultures, and nations to spread the Good News of Jesus Christ to every corner of the earth.

To join us in reaching the world,
visit **rhema.org/wpc** or call **1-866-312-0972**.

Always on.

For the latest news and information on products, media, podcasts, study resources, and special offers, visit us online 24 hours a day.

rhema.org

Free Subscription!

Call now to receive a free subscription to *The Word of Faith* magazine from Kenneth Hagin Ministries. Receive encouragement and spiritual refreshment from . . .

- *Faith-building articles from Kenneth W. Hagin, Lynette Hagin, Craig W. Hagin, and others*
- *"Timeless Teaching" from the archives of Kenneth E. Hagin*
- *Feature articles on prayer and healing*
- *Testimonies of salvation, healing, and deliverance*
- *Children's activity page*
- *Updates on Rhema Bible Training College, Rhema Bible Church, and other outreaches of Kenneth Hagin Ministries*

Subscribe today for your free *Word of Faith*!

1-888-28-FAITH (1-888-283-2484)

rhema.org/wof